Expect the Unexpected

KUM KUM SEN

DIANA KAUSHIK

ROSAMA FRANCIS

Printed in India

ISBN: 978-93-6045-583-5

First Printing, 2024

IndiePress

A division of Nasadiya Technologies Private Ltd.

Koramangala, Bangalore

Karnataka-560029

http://indiepress.in/

Edited by Anagha Somanakoppa

Typeset by Pagemajik

Book Cover designed by Sankhasubhro Nath

Publishing Consultant – Samyuktha Prasanan

A special thanks to my son-in-law, Benjamin Su, Directing Animator at Pixar and a Marvel Cover Artist, for all the illustrations; to Anu, for typing most of my chapters; and to my daughter Runa for her help and constant encouragement.

About the Authors

Three women; we met in Coorg on a holiday. We came from different backgrounds, but a common faith—Christianity.

Even though women do not necessarily 'get along' famously on a trip, we were OK; we survived, and we gave each other space. The idea of doing something together originated there, in the pristine surroundings of the resort we were staying in, and this is the bond that will keep us together.

In the book, "Women Who Run With The Wolves," Clarissa Pinkola Estes reveals how within every woman lives a wild woman, longing to do something out of the ordinary, a sort of ageless knowing. Still, only a select few are able to rejoice and express their truth unabashedly and knowingly.

So here we are, sharing our stories, emotions, intuitive wisdom, and lust, to reveal a bit of ourselves to the world. Rose and Diana, your stories are wonderful. I hope they can inspire other women to be more in control of their lives, to not lose their feminine instinctual psyche or fear being stepped upon or cornered in any way.

Rose was born into a Syrian Christian family in the 60s in Pune, Maharashtra. She had a blissfully carefree childhood. Her father served in the armed forces. With each move, he transformed the surroundings with beautiful gardens, butterflies, sparrows, and rabbits. They lost this wonderful man when she was seventeen. Even though life seemed incomprehensible, she worked hard and topped her class. This profound loss taught her to meet future challenges with strength and courage. She married, had two children, and started her career as a teacher. In her late 40s, she discovered Vipassana, a Buddhist Meditation system. She then ventured out of her comfort zone to establish herself as a leadership coach and in this, she says, she has found her true calling.

She presently practices Falun Dafa, an ancient Spiritual practice. Ever since life has been a blessing.

Diana was born into a close-knit Christian family in Nagpur, Maharashtra. They were God-fearing, loving, caring, and supportive of each other. Her father was the sole breadwinner, and her mother was the homemaker. Obedience, righteousness, and spirituality were what she stood for

Diana married twice; the first at an early age due to unexpected family circumstances, and the second was an inter-caste marriage to an Indian Air Force officer. She has two children from her first marriage, both settled in Hong Kong. She is presently based in Jaipur. Diana provides for herself by owning and running a school that has just been sold. She holds the title of President of the Jaipur Goan Association.

She strives to be a "Blessing in Disguise" to the needy in Jaipur in her own small ways.

I cherish my friendship with her. She has indeed moved on and come a long way, becoming a surer, more fearless, free-roaming, free-thinking woman of her time.

The Greek philosopher Heraclitus felt that consulting our own experiences and intuition is a wonderful way to gain insight, and she has done exactly that!

Lastly, I **Kum Kum** was born and raised in Rajasthan and went to school and college in Jaipur. My first job was also in Jaipur, till I got married and left the town for good, only to come back years later.

Jackie, my father, was in the IPS; Dulcie, my mother, was a keen homemaker and a cook. She successfully ran a Jaipur-style cloth printing business on the premises for a short while. Christmas was truly a big event with friends and family when my mother made Christmas cakes of 72 eggs to start with! The cakes became smaller and smaller in number as the years went by. She helped found All Saints Church School and Balika Sadan, a home for destitute girls.

I led a simple and protected life. Life was simpler in those days. After a short stint in Delhi, where I did a Nursery & Primary Teachers Training, I got a job in my Alma Mater, M.G.D, for a handsome salary of Rs.500/-. The great Miss Lutter, our principal, interviewed me. I worked here only for a year. After that, I led a diplomat's life, moving every three years until my husband and I returned to Delhi. Here, I volunteered for the Indian Cancer Society, earlier on with the Canadian Cancer Society in Ottawa. Since this seemed to be my passion, I also held two paid jobs in a couple of hospitals in Delhi. It was a very satisfying time and occupation, but then I had to move to Jaipur, where I had built a house. I spent ten years in my beautiful home till unexpected circumstances brought me back to Delhi.

You see, I have moved house only 14 times in my life!

Contents

Chapter 1

To Be(lieve) Or Not To Be(lieve)

**- Kum Kum Sen, Diana Kaushik
and Rosama Francis:
Our Spiritual Journeys**

"If men were to come out of their self-limiting veils that cover your eyes, what glorious revelation he will see in every faith."

Ghalib

"Ye zameen jab na thi, ye jahan jab na tha, chand suraj na the, aasman jab na tha, tab na tha kuch yahan, tha magar- tu hi tu-tu hi tu- Allah hoo."

(When Nothingness reigned, You were there!)

"Her sheh pukarti hai, kay tu parwar digar hain. Patta patta, teri kudrat ka pata deta hein."

(The Universe and every leaf in it, reflects your glory and existence).

When Nusrat Fateh Ali Khan belts this number, his face depicts a frenzy, a passion, a certain madness and an immense sense of belief that only such a one, a specially gifted, can have.

Perhaps this is what my father meant to say, if we came upon him, reading his Bible in the early hours of the morning. This private reading and conversation with the Almighty was a daily affair with him. He said, this was an immeasurable help to him to face the day and the challenges that came with it.

To the seeker, Nusrat says, *"Jis ki pahauch jaha talak, uske liye wahi hai tu (Where anyone can reach or seek; for them, i.e. where You are)."*

Nusrat then ends the qawwali, "All the creation searches for you. You are manifest in all dimensions, O Peerless One, Oh King of Kings."

Similarly, the very first verse in the Bible begins like this: "In the beginning, when God created the Universe, the earth was formless and desolate-----" Here, the Bible does not even try to explain if God existed, from all eternity past. It just states this as a fact. God is one, who desires a personal relationship with us. He is Spirit, infinite in every way and unchanging at all times. He is all powerful, all knowing, infinitely wise, infinitely loving, and pure. He is also merciful, for His love IS unconditional for us. His mercy comes before his wrath, so that through His mercy, you may experience the suffering of existence

On the other hand, Khuswant Singh talks about evolving a personal religion for himself, whereby he quotes, *"Dhundta firta hun main, ai Iqbal, apne aap ko; aap hi goya musafir, aap hi manzil hun main"* (O Iqbal, I go about everywhere looking for myself. As if I were the wayfarer as well as the destination). No religion, he says, evoked much enthusiasm in his mind. By the time India gained independence, he had openly declared himself an agnostic. He felt that religion was an opiate for the masses, [this opinion is perfectly depicted in the book "City of Joy"] and for those who had the courage to think for themselves, a new set of beliefs needed to be brought about. He says the honest truth being that we do not know where we come from, whether or not there is divine purpose in our existence, nor do we know where we will go when we die. I just love his motto, that he has coined for modern India.

"Work is worship but worship is not work."

Khuswant Singh suggests that apart from chanting mantras, reading scriptures, and spending hours and hours in prayers and meditation, every person should set aside at least one hour of the day for social service, from which he or she derives no personal benefits.

Ella Wheeler Wilcox said, "So many Gods, so many creeds, so many parts that wind and wind, when just an act of being kind is all that a sad world needs."

A favorite actor of mine, Akshay Kumar suggests, "Instead of staring at a candle for hours in the form of 'Meditation' why not give time to someone else, help someone, do a service, help the needy?"

You can also do both, for example my mother Dulcie, a regular Church goer and believer, also put in many years of dedicated service for many neglected stratas of society.

Francis S Collins, the Head of the Human Genome Project, believes in a God who can listen to prayers and who cares about our souls. For Collins, Science does not conflict with the Bible, Science enhances it! He argues that belief in God can be an entirely rational choice. One can be a rigorous scientist, and a person who believes in a God who takes personal interest in each one of us. It must be examined with the heart, the mind, and the soul—and the mind must find a way to embrace both realms.

> "Faith consists in believing when it is beyond the power of reason to believe. It is not enough that a thing be possible for it to be believed."
>
> - Voltaire

Many argue that no wonder there are atheists in this world as terrible things have been done in the name of religion. While they proclaim the goodness of God, organized religions have violated their own beliefs by their perpetual violence and prejudice. Otherwise, why would a loving God allow suffering in this world?

We have been given free will, the ability to do as we please. Sister Shivani of the Brahma Kumari reiterates this in her various talks. We use this free will to frequently disobey the moral law. The tragedy of a young child killed by a drunk driver, of the innocent man dying on a battlefield, of children losing the limbs in mine fields, or of women being raped can hardly be blamed on God.

Deepak Chopra lists a few rational, yet not too skeptical responses to our sense of beliefs.

- Faith is personal. It does not need to be justified to anyone.

- You feel faith, you experience it- you participate in it- you can't judge it from the outside.

- Faith is a way of exploring reality, but it does not have to pass scientific testing.

- Faith looks beyond physical appearances.

- Faith is about meaning. About new possibilities.

Martin Luther King Junior says, "Faith is taking the first step even when you don't see the whole staircase."

Even Sartre, the French atheist, said on his deathbed, "I do not feel that I am a product of chance, a speck of dust in the Universe, but rather someone who is expected, prepared, prefigured, in short, a being whom a creator God could have put here."

Rafiq Zakaria in his DISCOVERY OF GOD concluded, "Despite the hammer blows inflicted by the most renowned intellectuals on the belief in the existence and the unity of God in the eighteenth and nineteenth centuries, followed by the unspeakable horrors the twentieth century witnessed, shaking that belief, God has managed to survive."

Grace is understood to be a spontaneous gift from God to people. Generous, free, totally undeserved, and unexpected. This is the love, favor, and blessing from the Almighty. We have to be empty, ready to receive this love and grace.

"Miracles come in moments. Be ready and willing."

- Wayne Dyer

Let's see what Diana has to say about this:

It was a blessing by default to be born into a close knit Christian family. I just took all this for granted, living my life like a running stream of a river.

The second time around in my wedded life, to make things work, and believing that it would make my bond stronger with my husband, I became passive about my Christian beliefs, while actively practicing a ritualistic Hindu way of life, including a change of name. From Diana I became Shikha!

Prayers were offered with a genuine approach, but perhaps Karma had started the cycle of payback time!

My children from my first marriage put pressure on me to change, rethink my faith and to instill a sense of discipline in my day to day life.

I had become a wreck, my strength and confidence was waning, and my heart was sore. It was here that I remembered a Sufi's saying, "When the world pushes you to your knees, you're in the perfect position to pray."

I prayed then, to the Saviour, The Forgiver, The Most Powerful, to give me back my health, strength, confidence, self love, self esteem, and happiness.

With a passage of time, and with a complete sense of Surrender, I bounced back to my original self. The caring, confident, cheerful, calm and loving Diana that I once was.

It is not only important to cherish love, but to cherish LOVE unconditionally, which happens only with the ALMIGHTY.

Let's see what Rose has to say about this:

Born into a Christian family, I experienced a vibrant childhood filled with frequent relocations due to my father's service in the Indian Air Force. As a family we were never practicing Christians. We were aware of the drawbacks of organized religion, hence we stayed away from it. My father's green thumb transformed our surroundings into breathtaking gardens teeming with birds, butterflies, and buzzing bees. My siblings and I delighted in playful rabbits and the magical transformations of caterpillars into butterflies, but I always felt a quest for something more.

Tragedy struck at seventeen when my father died of a sudden heart attack just before my 12th-grade exams. This profound loss deepened my search for meaning and peace. Over the next twenty years, I explored various practices, including Reiki, Yoga, Sudarshan Kriya, and several meditation techniques, eventually finding Vipassana, which provided a glimpse of what I sought.

Years later, my journey led me to Falun Dafa, a profound spiritual practice that brought the peace and equanimity I had been seeking since childhood. This practice has become the cornerstone of my spiritual cultivation, helping me understand the true meaning of life.

Chapter 2

The Art of Happiness
- Kum Kum

"Seeking happiness outside ourselves is like waiting for sunshine in
a cave facing north."

- Tibetan Saying

When I read somewhere or heard someone say that the goal of their life is to 'be happy' it sounded too simplistic, almost embarrassing! Isn't happiness a butterfly, which when pursued, is always beyond our grasp, but if you will sit down quietly, may alight upon you? So how do we pursue it, or make it a goal of your life? For this familiar, obscure, paradoxical object of desire, this happiness is elusive like the butterfly.

Luca and Francesco Cavelli-Sforza say, "Happiness does not come automatically. It is not a gift that good fortune bestows us and a reversal of fortune takes back."

What then is our vision of happiness? Only 'good times' and prosperity or contentment; and a 'self centered satiation?'

Sociologists define happiness as "The degree to which a person evaluates the overall quality of his or her present life as-a-whole, positively."

"Does our happiness depend only on our external circumstances and resources or is it the radiation of joy over one's entire existence or over the most vibrant part of one's active past, one's actual present, or one's conceivable future?"the philosopher Robert Misrahi puts it.

For St. Augustine, happiness is "a rejoicing in the truth."

For Marx it is about " growth through work."

For a French actress, happiness "is eating a plate of spaghetti" or "walking in the snow under the stars."

The word happiness is so overused, so much so that those who use it frequently, do not know what it evokes.

For some, it's a bit of shopping, or a lot of it. It is actually 'retail therapy,' for it provides momentarily joy and diversion.

According to the media, eating chocolate, a burger, or buying an expensive bag, shoes, lipstick, mobile, or even a shampoo are all sources of happiness!

Some may feel 'happy' seeing a 'sad' movie. Some may feel sad even in an otherwise happy situation; for example, a vacation, party, or relationship. The paradox is for all to see. It's been scientifically proven that listening to 'sad' songs lifts the mood and spirit.

In the movie, 'Inside Out' the emoji 'Sadness' says she is of utmost importance as without her the emoji 'Joy,' would not know her true worth!

Sadness and adversity enrich human character.

As per the Bhagavad Gita:

The soul that with a constant calm,

Takes sorrow and takes joy indifferently,

Lives in the life undying!

Is it all about a few pleasant sensations, an intense pleasure, an eruption of joy, a sunny day, a beautiful sunset, a walk in nature, a child's smile, a hug from a grandchild, or any other magical moment in our day to day existence? Happiness is surely not a short pleasurable feeling, a fleeting emotion, or a mood, but an optimal state of being, a lasting fulfillment. Happiness is also how we interpret the world. Since while it may be difficult to change the world, it is always possible to change the way we look at it!

"We read the world wrong and say that it deceives us."

- Rabindranath Tagore

In the movie 'Highway,' Veera, the protagonist, experiences pure bliss, joy, and happiness when she sits atop a mountain summit looking out over a vast horizon, from the walk at night through snow under a starry sky, and the babbling brooks she comes across. In spite of her bondage, she experiences total freedom and harmony with the world and herself. This serene wilderness is new to her and she doesn't want it to end, even if she has the choice to return to her family and home. She simply IS, here and NOW, free and happy. This moment is liberated from her painful past, and is not burdened with plans for the future. This moment was to her a state of GRACE, which was soon going to end, when she would go back to her conflicting and unhappy state of mind. She does go back only to REALIZE that money and comfort cannot provide never ending peace and happiness.

Richard Layard of the Delhi School of Economics states, "We have more food, more clothes, more cars, bigger houses, more central heating, more foreign holidays, a shorter working week, nice work, and above all, better health. Yet we are not happier!"

Happiness is bound up with distress when we lack adequate inner resources to sustain certain basic elements of 'Sukha,' the joy of being alive, that we do have an ability to flourish, and the feeling that we are APART from the Universe, and not an integral part of it. Then we experience 'Dukha' or pain. Ignorance, in the Buddhist perspective, is not stupidity, but just the inability to recognize the true nature of things.

Even if one agrees that suffering and pain can bring about a change, a transformation, no one seeks out ways to feel miserable and unhappy. Of course, the 'Meena Kumari Complex' is something else which refers to a certain feeling of anguish and depression for no reason at all. Here, it is about a selective state of being, a creativity or a poetic insurgence that would naturally emerge out of it.

In Shantaram, one of my favorite books, Karla says that those who are unable to feel 'sad,' get depressed. This then is that thriving, that creative urge, that surrender, that happens when someone feels sad; but not depressed. It is that aloneness; not loneliness, that solitude; not boredom, that desire; not weariness, that hope; not doubt, a fulfillment and deep down of a different kind. That suffering; never unhappiness!

So how do we go from suffering to freedom? The Bible says, "Come to me, all you who are weary and burdened, and I will give you rest."

Mathew Ricard says that happiness is a skill that can be cultivated.

Can we be transformed? Can we control our minds? Can we polish this skill like we do with dancing, singing, cooking, cricket, or chess? Can we inculcate happiness into our lives?

Yes we can:

Simplify, wrote the American moralist Henry David Thoreau. This is easier said than done. We ourselves make our lives so complicated and cluttered. The T.V. or any other social media envelopes us with words, sounds, pictures, gossip, and unnecessary options. This distracts us and may lead to mental confusion. If we have to leave our homes in an emergency, which 2 objects would you pick? I would like to pick them all up! That's how attached we are to our prized possessions. If we work on this we take a step toward a happier life.

A daily **Meditation** or **Introspection**—an inward looking practice or gaze. Watching our thoughts arise and move on and bathing in this state of serenity and simplicity is most fruitful.

An **Awareness** that suffering is an intrinsic part of our daily lives. The first line of 'Road Less Traveled' states, "Life is difficult." The

Buddhists say that in this cycle of death and rebirth, no place, not even one the size of a needle's point, is exempt from suffering.

There is always a **Choice**. Even though suffering and pain is inevitable, stress and unhappiness is not. We have to work on this inner well being."

"The wise man has nothing left to expect or to hope for. Because he is entirely happy, he needs nothing. Because he needs nothing, he is entirely happy!"

Bhutan is the first and only country in the world to have a government edict that Gross National Happiness (G.N.H.) is more important than Gross National Product (G.N.P.). The principles of G.N.H. emphasizes selfless service and the search for enlightenment as a core value of this unique Buddhist Kingdom.

This **Inner Peace** does not come easy. It needs tremendous effort and determination. Small things cause us distress. A broken nail, a flat tyre, traffic snarls, the maid not turning up, no internet, an unpleasant neighbor, weather issues, all may cause deep frustration and displeasure. What might the tragic events then do to us? They may completely overwhelm us, destroy us and our state of mind.

We see 'I' and 'Mine' in many situations of our daily lives. It's my name, my car, my home, my children, my possessions,my friends, my wife! This erroneous '**duality**' causes a lot of mental frustration and possessiveness, and suffering.

A mere consciousness and application will help a great deal to find our more natural and happier state of being.

Make peace with our **Emotions**. When a painful emotion strikes us, accept it and look at it head on, identifying the immediate thoughts. FIX an inner gaze on them, and gradually diffuse and dissolve them.

With the help of experience we can deal with negative emotions before they surface. We can see them coming. We can then work on mastering our afflictive thoughts, moods, and disposition. We can be more open to the world.

"Umeed pay duniya kaayam hai." Never ever lose **Hope**! Hope is defined by psychologists as the conviction that one can find the means and attain one's goals and develop the motivation necessary to do so. It's never too late or hopeless or lost; always an alternate solution, whether realistic or spiritual.

In the movie 'Pursuit of Happyness,' coming to terms is not an option for the protagonist. He struggles and juggles his time and frugal resources to find success one day, but never for a moment losing hope or compromising on the love and care he gives his son as a single parent, even though they are on the road one day, and homeless another.

Happiness is an infectious trait. Take time to build quality relationships with supportive people to catch the right infection. If you have to be physically around someone out of compulsion, learn to switch off mentally at the very moment they start to say something negative. Remember that if your happiness rests on having happy people in your life, surely you also have to be one such person for those who have you in you in their lives.

Be **Kind** to yourself rather than overly self critical or perfectionistic.

"I thought the phrase 'Love Yourself' would mean something extra special to people who are harsh on themselves."

- Jimin of the B.T.S. group

\# **Appreciate** what you already have, rather than focussing only upon what you still desire.

"Milta toh bahut kuch hai is zindagi mein, par hum ginti usi ki karte hai jo haasil na ho saka."

- Gulzaar

\# Lastly, work on being **Humble**. It is indeed a forgotten value in today's world.

The above mentioned suggestions are all valid and helpful in themselves. However, if at a time when we feel we are struggling in life, it is advisable to reach out to mental health professionals. This is indeed a brave and bold step to take.

"Happiness cannot be traveled to, owned, earned, worn, or consumed. Happiness is the spiritual experience of living every minute with love, grace, and gratitude"

- Diies Willey

Chapter 3

Look Good, Feel Good
- Kum Kum

"The door to success swings outward not inward!"

- Robin Sharma

It would be a complete lie to say that good looks or rather looking good is not of utmost importance in this day and age. But of course, personality, character, smartness, and intelligence is far more important than just good looks.

I have been a member of the Indian Cancer Society (Delhi Branch) now for many years. The organization is dedicated to creating awareness about cancer, providing emotional support to cancer patients and also providing funds for the under-privileged. It is also involved in rehabilitation of cancer survivors, registry, research, and education. The people behind it are focused, devoted, innovative, and quite incredible. They too suggest that to feel good, confident, worthy, and healthier, every one surviving cancer has to make that extra effort to 'look good.' They make the following suggestions:

- Prosthetic Bras: For women who have undergone a mastectomy, this is a must to look confident. It's important to keep the body and spine balanced, otherwise the latter may be affected forever.

- Wigs: Wigs for women who lose their hair after chemotherapy help to give them that extra edge to look good and therefore, feel good.

- Scarves: Scarves tied innovatively around the head and neck not only adds style and glamor but also cover the head. Many videos are available online for this.

- Wholesome Diet: A good and balanced diet helps to heal the body quicker. A diet rich in protein makes one stronger and more energetic.

- Regular Walks and Exercises: This is of utmost importance too.

Rekha Gulabani, a cancer survivor, a favorite of mine and active member of Indian Cancer Society, believes in empowering the survivors. She says, *"Sahil ki taraf kashti kar le. Toofan ke thapede sahna kya. Tu aap hi apna majhi ban. Maujo ke sahare chalna kya (Why be lashed by the waves? Face your boat towards the shore. Learn to navigate, and not be rocked so)!"*

Robin Sharma, my favorite motivational guide says, "You can't be great at work until you feel great. You can't make someone feel good about themselves until YOU feel good about yourself. And you can't be a source of Positive Energy, if you have no energy."

Perhaps the following **TIPS** might help you in this journey:

- Often people have remarked, "Why do you need to go to the gym? Do you really need to pump iron? Isn't it only for the young and trendy?"

Here's my take: Exercise, be it walking, yoga, swimming, or gymming, it will make you look better, healthier, and happier. Okay, forget about looking better. What about being stronger, more energetic, better balanced on your feet? Getting into good physical condition is one of the smartest moves you can make. Staying fit will even make you happier! NOTHING LIKE A GOOD WORKOUT. Our cardiovascular system works better. More blood is sent to the active skeletal muscles. There is a definitive glow to the skin. Sleep is improved and energy increases. So, go ahead, hit the gym, whatever your age might be. After a certain age, getting a stronger pair of legs is all you can ask for.

- Keep moving, this keeps you young. Walk, 'JUST DO IT.'

Dr. Kirti of Peak Performance (Physiotherapy and Sports Rehab) in Bangalore advises that the only way for older people to stay fit and active is constant mobility. Even while watching your favorite T.V. program, take a break, walk around a bit, do a few stretches, have a sip or two of water and then return to your seat.

- Maintain a regular routine of skin care.

- Never wait till you are really thirsty. Stay hydrated.

- Use sunscreen daily before stepping out.

- Work on your strongest feature. Concentrate on what God has blessed us with.

> "It is not a lip or eye we beauty call. But the joint force
> and full result of all."

> - Alexander Pope

- Nourish your body; Nourish your soul. Eat well. A balanced diet will go a long way to keep us healthy and well. Eat until you are 80% full. Then stop. Gluttony, one of the seven deadly Sins, is committed by us more than once in our lives.

- Dress well. Don't follow fashion; cultivate your own style.

- Try out a new hairstyle. This does wonders for our overall look and confidence.

- Maintain a healthy weight. A positive personal appearance is a fast, effective way to boost self confidence and overcome anxiety regarding comfort, confidence, and acceptance.

- Life is good. Take the required supplements.

- Get regular medical checkups done.

- Smile always. By smiling, you're conditioning your brain to feel happy and think happy thoughts.

- Learn how to massage your face correctly. Oils for face are aplenty in the market. This increases circulation which adds a healthy glow, and relaxes muscle tension to help reduce wrinkles.

- The same for a good body massage. Along with improved blood circulation, it also helps with joint pain, energy and a 'feel good' in general.

Chapter 4

Healthy Aging

- Kum Kum

"Age is a question of mind over matter; if you don't mind, it doesn't matter!"

- Mark Twain

In December 2013, my husband's batch of Mayo College, Ajmer, celebrated their 50th Reunion. Time stood still as they were transported back to childhood memories of yesteryears spent together in carefree abandon. The 'boys' had so much fun. Everyone got along famously. My highlight of that evening was meeting Tinu Anand, the maker of one of my favourite Amitabh Bachchan's movies, 'Shahenshah.' He was as friendly and approachable as he was 50 years ago and he looked good too. His lovely wife entertained us with incredible Bollywood dance moves. She proved to be an attractive gray haired bundle of energy!

We were a colorful mix of retired generals, officials, judges, economists, businessmen, a golfer, a DJ (who came specially from Canada), and a movie director. 50 years! A long time, but not long enough not to look good and feel 'forever young.' In the song 'Forever Young,' the Canadian Tenors sing "May you grow up to be righteous, may you grow up to be true. May your hands always be busy, may your feet always be swift. May your heart always be joyful, your song always be sung. And may you stay forever young!"

So, then why are some individuals so outwardly altered by time and others not? Why is there a discrepancy between chronological age and biological age? Why do some of us look fit and energetic and others tired, unhealthy, and pale? Andrew Weil (M.D.) believes that the answer has to do with a complex interaction of genetics and environment. Aging is a continuous and necessary process of change that begins with conception, but how do we maximize health and happiness? Why do some of us manage to keep the magic wand lit up and others let it slip away so easily?

> Age is not reversible. We all know that, but it can be arrested to a great degree.
>
> What is 'Age?' Henry Wordsworth Longfellow says:
>
> "For age is opportunity no less

Than youth itself, though in another dress,

And as the evening twilight fades away,

The sky is filled with stars invisible by day."

The age issue is tricky because if you think of 60 as young, you'll be a young 60. If you believe 80 means decrepit, your body and mind is already working to accommodate your belief.

The hard fact is that aging will bring about unpleasant changes, among them aches and pains, decreased vigor, healing ability, less sensory acuity, muscle tone, bone density, and sexual energy. It will also bring about memory defects, wrinkles, loss of beauty, friends, family, and independence, and an increased reliance on doctors, and pills, and social isolation. In the western world, many old people die of S.A.D. (Seasonal affective disorders). Because of the extremely cold climate, going outdoors, breathing in fresh air, and getting adequate sunlight becomes impossible. The skin then becomes pale, mind depressed, and body weak. So yes, aging can bring frailty and suffering, but what else does it do?

To age gracefully, let us understand that 'old' is synonymous with 'good.' Why does old cheese, wine and old whiskey all taste better? Why are antiques more sought after? Why are old books and pianos treasured more? What is it that moves us in the presence of old trees? Let us then look for qualities in these and the corresponding qualities in people. Let us safely assume that age does bring about depth and richness of experience, complexity of being, serenity, wisdom, and its own kind of power and grace!

To the extent that we think about the inevitability of aging and death, we usually have great trepidation—a sentiment captured well by Psalm 71: 9. "Do not cast me off in old age, when my strength fades do not forsake me."

Often when we see the silent darkness of old age, we miss the million sparks of life still present. The poet Zelda once wrote,

> "Life's magic will never return,
>
> it won't return.
>
> Suddenly in my house, the sun
>
> is a living thing,
>
> and the table with its bread—
>
> gold.
>
> And the flower and the cups—
>
> gold.
>
> And the sadness?
>
> Even there—
>
> radiance."

Some More Thoughts on Ageing (Growing Old Gracefully):

- We are who we are. We should concentrate on being our authentic selves.

- Happily, most of us will not have to age the way our parents and grandparents did. We know about the options of better medicines and other facilities, to somewhat arrest the outward signs of aging. We understand the importance of physical activity and the management of stress!

- Our attitude and approach to life is needless to say of utmost importance. Not only can we alter our outward circumstances by changing our attitude, we can also alter our attitude by changing our circumstances!

- The bloom of youth is of course wonderful, but we owe it to ourselves to maintain these qualities attributed to youth—enthusiasm, vitality, and fitness.

  ACCEPT- Aging will happen. Denial of aging and the attempt to fight it is counterproductive, a major obstacle to aging gracefully.

  ADAPT- As your body changes, you grow into a more seasoned but still exquisite version of yourself.

  ADJUST- Adjust to the new and renewed you.

- Work on your body's balance. As we age, we are more prone to falling and therefore, the importance of practicing a variety of Yoga Asanas cannot be stressed enough. Yoga can help with strength and balance, thereby walking better and preventing injury.

Helen, the famous dancer of yesteryears has taken to Pilates very recently at the age of 85. She says that once she stopped exercising, her balance was being affected, and she was forced to take up the walking stick. Now she suggests Pilates for all age groups.

The body will feel and be that much stronger, flexible, and yielding with Yoga. Aches and pains will reduce. The aim of Yoga is to calm the chaos of conflicting impulses. Meditation combined with Yoga is a bonus.

- Mr. R.M. Lala who is also J.R.D. Tata's Biographer suggests, "Cherish every moment of your life and be grateful you are there to see them."

- Live in the Present. Since the past is history, the future a mystery, this present is all we have, a gift from God. Live it!

- Develop a willingness to try and explore new things. Taking up new hobbies, interests, and activities goes a long way in keeping us busy and involved. J.R.D. Tata, I believe, started skiing at 40, and went on for many years after that.

- Forgive others. Forgive and forget. I agree this is easier said than done, but for our own well being, we have to constantly work at this.

- Worry, fault finding, resentment, and regret—all of these accelerate the negative aspects of aging. It shows on the face! So beware!

- Remember, stress is a choice. So however tough life feels, take solace in the company of family and friends. Stay positive. Stay active. Fight it out. I promise you, you will stay 'Forever Young"

"If there is a cure, what good is discontent? If there is no cure, what good is discontent?"

- Regrets make you sick! Wipe out two words from your vocabulary, "If only." Instead use, "Next time."

- Take on any spiritual path, one that gives you succor and peace of mind. We have all felt God's love at some point. It might have been in a book, a friend, or in nature, right?

- Downsize. Give away valuables. See the joy on the faces that receive it. By giving, you get richer.

Keep the ego under wraps. A previous Captain of the Indian Cricket team said that ego is only good when it adds to your motivation level. Along with wisdom may come a rigidity, a lack of trust, and a more active ego. A young doctor friend reminded me that he wished his elders were a little more trusting, and open to newer and younger ideas.

Recently, at the Jaipur Literature Festival, thousands of us got the chance to see and listen to Gulzar recite poetry, stories, experiences, and anecdotes of his life. A very young 89 years old, he is springy, fit, and fine. With a poetic brilliance, he shone like a diamond. All were in awe of him, loving him, and appreciating him fully.

A very strange comparison, but Arnold Schwarzenegger too advises to always keep busy and active with new ideas, projects, and meetings. An active mind and body will keep us "Forever Young."

Shyam Benegal, also 89, who is married to my cousin Nira, says, "Life treats you the way you treat life." To keep happy and fit, he continues to do whatever he wants to. Reading and of course, filmmaking are his main focus. He was a regular swimmer till he was 70. What has helped him tremendously in his life is having an organized lifestyle, his meals on time and controlling smoking and drinking. He also suggests not to worry needlessly. Just don't worry. Be happy!

On a lighter note, "Don't take life too seriously, you'll never escape it alive anyway."

Chapter 5

Love, Longing, and Loss

- Diana

"Love gives nothing but itself, and takes nothing but from itself. Love does not possess, nor would it be possessed. Do not think that you can direct the course of love, for love, if it finds you worthy, directs your course. Love has no other desire but to fulfill itself."

- Khalil Gibran

In the grand design of creation, every life is woven with infinite care, each thread infused with divine purpose, and every hue reflecting the depth of human experience. This is my story, a narrative spun from the delicate fibers of joy, the stark void of loss, and the unyielding quest for love.

My First Marriage:

In my first marriage, I was like a lone gardener who took care of my husband's needs. I was taken care of financially, sure. I only had to give good food and a warm bed in return. Is that enough, though? The flowers of love were not blooming in this garden of duty. I felt like I was on an empty boat, floating on an ocean of indifference. My soul longed for the harbor of love, echoing the psalmist's cry: "As the deer pants for streams of water, so my soul pants for you, my God." (Psalm 42:1)

Enter: A Love That Soared and Crashed:

Then Sqn Ldr. Seth came into my life like a comet streaking across the night sky. His quick decisions, like a skydiver falling, showed how smart he was as a worker. But his personal life was like a plane caught in a tailspin: an illicit liaison, while still married to his first wife, caused his being cut off from the Indian Air Force and brought his free spirit to the ground. But I believed:

> Through Love all that is bitter will be sweet.
>
> Through Love all that is copper will be gold.
>
> Through Love all dregs will turn to purest wine.
>
> Through Love all pain will turn to medicine.
>
> Through Love the dead will all become alive.

Our Roller Coaster Life Together:

Even though Seth's past was a mess, I stood by him because I had faith in the power of love to heal. I became his anchor, the steady presence that helped him through life's storms. Over time, he regained his honor, earning the respect of both society and his family, who had turned their backs on him before. Our journey together was a testament to the scripture: "Love bears all things, believes all things, hopes all things, endures all things." (1 Corinthians 13:7)

The Struggle with Faith and Identity:

As our lives intertwined, his family rejoiced in a religious conversion that never took root in my heart. The gnawing guilt of forsaking my faith began to consume me, even as I balanced the myriad responsibilities of our shared existence with unwavering resolve. In hindsight, perhaps that was the fatal flaw. For different reasons, women don't notice red flags in men. I am still introspective about mine. Because those signs were there all along. For most of us, first impressions are very important, and we tend to have a very positive idea of our partner right away. This first impression shapes all the decisions we make in the future, and we only look for evidence that supports it. We also want to believe good things about our partner, so we don't pay attention to warning signs. Trust issues and the need to play the peacemaker can also make us ignore warning signs. But learn from my mistakes and remember how important it is to see these warning signs and put our well-being first in relationships.

The Downward Spiral:

In the quiet corners of my heart, a secret lay buried—my faith. The family was very proud because they thought they had successfully converted me to their religion. But deep down, their rituals and beliefs didn't change mine. When my faith was weakening, guilt tore at my soul. Life weaved its complicated web. Similar to my first marriage, I took on the role of caretaker, taking care of my family, our shared children, our finances, and business matters. Seth's old habits came back to the surface. His adventurous spirit demanded new horizons, and he flitted across cities and states for his adrenaline-fuelled pursuits, albeit for work. I followed suit and made frequent visits, enjoying short periods of being spoiled and pampered. I loved his homecomings during the four months he wasn't flying. Late-night revelry, friends prioritized over family, and my undivided attention became the rhythm of our existence.

He thoroughly enjoyed the constant movement and his confidence soared as he received billing from multiple schools, almost reaching a level of arrogance. Soon, the spark that used to get Seth excited faded. The thrill he sought—like the rush of a bungee jump—no longer found its echo in our relationship. I did everything I could to reignite the flame: I dressed how he liked, shared drinks, and danced until the wee hours of the morning. I loved being his versatile soulmate and felt lucky to be able to share these times with my husband. But fate had other plans. Little did I know, when he was away from home, his need for such a partner was quickly substituted by other women. So when duty called, Seth's attention shifted elsewhere. People admired his work in adventure sports and the way he acted around school directors and principals, who were often women. His uniform and Air Force background made him impossible to resist. His philandering ways returned. The cycle repeated. My yearning returned. Desperately making me want love and care and making my heart ask in silence, "Will I ever be enough?"

The Nail in the Coffin:

Destiny had different intentions. Seth had a natural gift for forming personal bonds. His warm and charming personality, thoughtful gestures (such as giving flowers or chocolates), captivated women.

They thought he only had eyes for them, completely unaware of how many others he was actually paying attention to. At first, I just saw this as something that came with his job in public relations. I noticed some small flirtations in his messages, but I chose to ignore them. Whenever faced with a confrontation, he would try to resolve the situation calmly. However, when his attempts at communication fell short, his anger would ignite, resulting in—no other way to put it— him physically assaulting me.

Things took a different turn when Seth formed a strong connection with a school principal in Hyderabad, who seemed to crave attention in general. His impressive track record of successful billing, combined with the positive feedback from students, made her confident in recommending him to other schools. Their friendship went beyond the norm, resulting in visits to her house while her sailor husband was away. Intimate relations flourished, driven by Seth's exaggerated stories of our lack of connection and commitments for the future.

There was a lot of commotion and confusion, and Seth refused to admit anything—even when presented with undeniable proof. Once again, history played out in a familiar pattern. Sixteen years ago, he had made a comparable error, wanting a future with a different lady. Once again, it was the principal. She viewed Seth as a caring individual, valuing his partner (me) and imagining herself in that position following the end of her marriage.

I gave him plenty of time, endured numerous discussions, but he just dismissed her as just a friend. His life choices were his own, and I found myself feeling quite lonely in the three-story school-residence we had built together. The tumultuous year of 2020 left me feeling overwhelmed and anxious, my thoughts swirling with uncertainty and the weight of the world, wanting to end it all with a leap off the terrace.

My Spiritual Awakening:

I found myself trapped in a negative atmosphere, feeling isolated and struggling. However, in the midst of the gloom, a faint ray of hope emerged as I rediscovered my spiritual connection. I found solace in prayer, dedicating countless hours to deep conversations and meditation with the divine. I yearned for respite from the anguish that consumed my heart, a constant ache that refused to subside. After what felt like an eternity, a sudden realization hit me—the anguish and jealousy that had consumed me had vanished. I made a promise to never abandon the belief that had carried me through every challenge.

And then, to my dismay, while I struggled with the overwhelming grief of losing my mother amidst the peak of the Covid crisis, Seth had moved in with his school principal 'friend' in her Dehradun home! It was then that his sister contacted me, after patiently waiting until the mandated cooling off period since our divorce filing. She earnestly implored me to reconsider getting a divorce, fully aware of her brother's true nature and my own hesitance to enter into another marriage. Ultimately, I decided to pursue a judicial separation. So even though I am still legally tied to him, I am entitled to the benefits provided by the Armed Forces. It felt as if it was the bare minimum he could provide, considering the two decades I had devoted to the idea of aging gracefully alongside the man I cherished. I longed for love and to be loved in return.

Now, I find comfort in my own cozy home, living life on my own way, and enjoying the peace of being alone. Meanwhile, Seth has been living his life in Dehradun, but recently, he has started to appreciate the importance of finding a genuine soulmate. I continue to come across his carefully planned, tactful gestures, as he slowly recognises my value and the assistance I provided him in his moments of difficulty.

I'd rather lose him than return to the toxicity of our past relationship. Instead, I'll cherish the love and companionship of my children, extended family, and friends.

A Call for Empathy and Awareness:

I long for people to not only empathize with women facing similar struggles and to admire the resilience of those who emerge from such situations, but also to extend sympathy to men who, for various reasons, descend into sociopathic behavior—a phenomenon worthy of deeper research. It's a tragedy for both of us to have our lives marred by this ordeal. Perhaps it would have been better if someone close to him, someone he admires, or his family had intervened and guided him towards the medical help he needed. And I say this because getting help from a psychologist or psychiatrist can help you deal with the problems that cause cheating, or emotional or physical violence towards your partner. Underlying issues such as unresolved traumas, personal insecurities, or mental health problems can be dealt with.

A lot of the time, I wonder why his family didn't help him sooner. They knew quite well of his tendencies and knew all too well about his past actions. However, because I was a Christian, they looked down on me, even though I had been his faithful life partner for twenty years and had helped him achieve a lot in his career. It's disheartening to realize that in our society, success is often attributed solely to the man, while blame is unfairly and almost always placed on women!

Given my strength of will, I am willing to extend a hand of friendship to him always. I'll stand by his side in times of emergency, offering support and assistance whenever he requires it. Because the fact of the matter is, you can't kill love. You can't even kill it with hate. You can kill in love and even loneliness, but never love itself. Every act of love, every moment of the heart reaching out, is a part of God. It is what we call God, and it can never die.

Chapter 6

Everyday Greatness/Everyday Creativity
- Kum Kum

"There are painters who transform the sun into a yellow spot, but there are others who with the help of their art and their intelligence, transform a yellow spot into the sun."

- Pablo Picasso

To Ponder: What is our Purpose? What is life asking from us? Let's face it. Life is not easy. The world is in commotion and all forecasts point towards more chaos ahead, more turbulence, more storms. So how do we function on a daily basis? Do we fill our lives with meaning and contribution? Do we contribute to anything, any cause, Community?

We are not all great heroes, writers, doctors, scientists, musicians, or athletes. We have to strive for another type of greatness—a quiet hidden one, an everyday greatness. It's a way of living, not a one time event. It's more about small and simple deeds; it's about humble motives and desires. So how can we become the Creative force of our lives and of our own futures?

The Bible describes 7 Deadly Sins to us:

1. Wrath (Anger)

2. Pride

3. Vanity

4. Envy

5. Gluttony (Greed)

6. Lust

7. Sloth

And again, there are 7 Deadly Sins according to Mahatma Gandhi:

1. Wealth without Work

2. Pleasure without Conscience

3. Knowledge without Character

4. Commerce without Morality

5. Science without Humanity

6. Religion without Sacrifice

7. Politics without Principles

Qualities like vision, compassion, humility, integrity, hard work, empathy, discipline, and innovation do provide us with the opposite of the above.

What would you choose?

Do you want more joy? More meaning? More self worth?

We have our own unique experience and talents. So let's work on these. Let's allow 'It' to happen!

> "Life is perpetually creative because it contains in itself
> that surplus which even overflows the boundaries of the
> immediate time and space, restlessly pursuing its adventure
> of expression in the varied forms of self- realization."
>
> - Rabindranath Tagore

It takes 21 days to make or break a habit.

Lets focus then on the following 21 tips:

1. It's a new Day. Wake up with gratitude in your heart, for all those who help you in your day to day life and for the Almighty. An ancient Persian saying explains this completely, "I wept because I had no shoes, until I saw a man who had no feet."

2. After jumping out of the bed, make it. Believe me, it's a fulfilling feeling.

3. A Prayer, Pranayam or a short Meditation is a good way to start the day with.

4. Do a few stretches for 10 minutes.

5. Pause, don't rush, If possible, make breakfast for yourself and for your family.

6. Two Japanese habits never fail to make you feel better. Cleaning the toilet and organizing your room. Japanese people believe that the mind will also be cleaned, thereby increasing chances of an increased fortune!

7. At work or on the road, try and exercise patience, compassion, charity etc. One good and kind word to a fellow worker, driver, or subordinate, goes a long way to enrich your own life.

8. Discover new and unique ways to be creative. Instead of executing road rage, try indulging in thinking activities. A new poem, song, joke, or something your spouse, child, or friend said that's worth remembering.

9. At home, try a new recipe, buy and arrange fresh flowers, paint a picture, sing a song, rearrange the furniture, change bedroom settings. Learn Ikebana.

10. In our day to day lives, think how we can give our hearts, time, talents, and energies to lighten the lives of others. A dear friend's mother always kept a great table. New snacks were offered to her children, their friends, grandchildren, and all visitors. She gave so much of herself to her family. My parents (Jackie and Dulcie) too, constantly gave so much of themselves to others, in kind words and deeds. They were involved with Church activities and other social services. All friends and family were welcome in their hearts and homes. They were humble, caring, involved, certainly imbibing values of everyday greatness.

11. Like my parents, learn to forgive. They were forgiving (almost to a fault) to friends and foes in general.

12. You have experiences and talents exclusive to you. TRUST THEM, USE THEM. All the resources are inside you.

13. Dream big, but take small steps. It's never too late. Life wants us to win. It sure does! We only need to do our part. Never give up! Only thing you might regret is not trying.

14. Invest in learning new skills. Learn to live a fuller life. Whatever your skills are. Practice, Polish, and Perform. Walk that extra mile.

15. In your daily life fight for a cause larger than yourself. Especially for women, who are experiencing the empty nest syndrome, there is nothing more satisfying and liberating.

16. Utilize your time well. Once gone it will never be back.

17. Practice compassion and kindness. Inderji, a flute player and a friend in Jaipur, always sat outside the Mandir, never inside. He said that compassion was the only thing worth practicing.

18. "Really, integrity is doing the right thing knowing that nobody is going to know whether you did it or not."

- Oprah Winfrey

This quality sustains every other principle of everyday greatness. How firmly are your feet planted? It means having your conscience and listening to it. There can be no happiness if your commitments and work don't reflect your values and what you stand for.

19. Innovate, imagine, and create. The opportunities of man are limited only by his imaginations. Learn, observe, and pursue. Unlock your own answers. Our own experiences and intuitions

will often help us to gain insight. Embrace paradox. How easily are few able to let go of one viewpoint in order to see a different one? As designer Rick Tendy puts it, "I never try to solve a problem by trying to solve it."

20. Find beauty in the mundane, not just the sublime. By finding humble patterns in our everyday life, we can prosper, create, and build. This can also help us in photography. Use your creative instincts well. For years, I saw images, designs, patterns, and faces in street signs, peeling paint, puddles of water, and floor designs. Light and dark in scenes and paintings but didn't use it creatively. Alas! Nevertheless, in the last 7 years, I have copied the works of ancient painters. Art like The Kiss, Picasso, Vincent Van Gogh. Absolutely enjoyed every moment of playing around with the vivid colors and designs.

21. Lastly, how well do we treat people? In this day and age when self centeredness and self appeasement is the way of the world, any good we do to help a person indeed will go a long way to get more out of life. Giving away valuables makes us richer!

"To ease another's heartache is to forget one's own."

- Abraham Lincoln

"Never hesitate to hold out your hand; Never hesitate to accept the outstretched hand of another."

- (Pope John XXIII)

Chapter 7

Anger Management

- Rose

"You can't see your reflection in boiling water; truth can't be seen in a state of anger, so always analyze before you finalize."

Unknown

Unraveling Anger:

One serene Sunday morning, the tranquility of my neighborhood was shattered by the piercing cries of a distressed young woman. Rushing to the scene, I found her in a state of utter turmoil, venting her frustrations by hurling objects at her own car. Concerned neighbors gathered below, their worry palpable as her distress escalated into an angry eruption, fueled by unmanaged emotions. Recognizing the urgency of the situation, I intervened, offering reassurance and guiding her back indoors.

Upon closer examination, it was evident that she was under the influence of substances, her senses clouded by intoxication. Understanding the gravity of her condition, I swiftly arranged for her transportation to the hospital, where she could receive the necessary treatment for substance addiction.

After engaging with her and her ex-boyfriend (who flew in to take care of her), I came to know that she had broken up with him three months back and while she was recouping from that trauma, her neighbor upstairs (another young guy) befriended her and supplied her with liquor and other intoxicants and had taken a fair amount of money and other things from her in her inebriated state.

Reflecting on the incident, it is apparent that her meltdown was a desperate plea for help. As she had no support structure as family or friends. Fortunately, she encountered individuals who rallied around her, facilitating access to the support and treatment she needed. As a result, her life trajectory began to ascend, highlighting the transformative impact of timely intervention and compassionate care.

I realized that her outburst was not an isolated incident but rather the culmination of numerous stressors that had accumulated over time. From the distressing memory of being asked to choose between her parents during a divorce settlement at the tender age of seven, to the recent heartbreak of a failed relationship three months prior, each small stressor had compounded, creating an unbearable burden that erupted on that fateful morning. This served as a poignant reminder of the importance of recognizing and addressing the underlying causes of distress, and offering support and intervention when it is needed most.

Today, after two years, she has embarked on a transformative journey. Through a meditation retreat and diligent self-work, she has found solace and inner peace. I'm delighted to share that she is now happily married to a fine gentleman, embracing a new chapter filled with love and contentment.

Unmet needs within anger is a complex emotion that is an integral part of the human experience. It is often misunderstood and wrongly perceived as a mere outburst of negativity. However, upon deeper reflection, anger is revealed to be a signal—a flag raised by unmet needs, waving desperately for attention.

Beneath the surface of many relationships lies an intricate dance of dynamics, where couples grapple with fundamental needs and desires. At the heart of these struggles often lies the quest for power and control, an ongoing negotiation of whose priorities take precedence and who holds sway in decision-making processes. It's a delicate balance between asserting one's autonomy and yielding to the needs of a partner.

Yet, intertwined with this quest for control is the pursuit of trust and closeness. Couples yearn to know if they can rely on each other, if their partner will stand by them through thick and thin, and if they can truly count on them to be there in times of need. It's about building a sense of security and emotional intimacy that forms the bedrock of a lasting bond.

Similarly, the battle for respect and recognition is ever-present. Couples seek validation of their worth and significance in each other's eyes. They crave acknowledgment of their contributions, validation of their feelings, and affirmation of their unique identity within the relationship. It's about feeling valued, appreciated, and seen for who they truly are.

Perhaps the most significant cause of anger is unmet needs. When our basic needs for safety, security, love, and belonging are not met, we may feel frustrated, angry, or resentful. These needs are universal and fundamental to human existence. When they are not met, we may feel a sense of powerlessness or helplessness, leading to feelings of anger or frustration. Understanding the connection between unmet needs and anger is crucial to managing anger effectively. When we experience anger, we must ask ourselves, "What need is not being met?" By identifying the unmet need, we can begin to address it, taking steps to meet the need in healthy, constructive ways. For example, if we feel angry because we are not receiving the love and attention we need from a partner or a colleague, we may lash out in passive-aggressive ways, such as giving the silent treatment. However, by recognizing that our need for love and attention is not being met, we can communicate our feelings openly and honestly with our partner/colleague, working together to find solutions that meet both of our needs. Or work towards fulfilling these needs from other sources so we can stay productive and healthy.

Similarly, if we are feeling angry because we are not receiving the respect we deserve at work, we may be tempted to lash out in aggressive ways, such as yelling or blaming others. However, by recognizing that our need for respect and recognition is not being met, we can communicate our feelings assertively, working with our colleagues and superiors to find ways to meet our needs effectively or look for a workplace that recognises your efforts without bias.

Anger is a powerful emotion that can range from mild irritation to intense fury. It is a natural response to frustration, injustice, or perceived threats. Often, anger is seen as a negative emotion, something to be avoided or suppressed. However, anger can also be a positive force for change, motivating individuals to take action and stand up for themselves and others.

Effectively managing anger begins with understanding our triggers. This involves training ourselves to take a step back, breathe deeply three times, and observe the sensations in our body. Once we've identified these sensations, we can pinpoint what specifically triggered our emotional response – whether it was a word, statement, or thought.

Next, we delve deeper to discern if our reaction was rooted in perception or reality. We then examine which of our fundamental needs – such as safety, security, love, or belonging – were not met in that moment. Armed with this awareness, we can seek out healthy ways to fulfill these needs.

This process may unfold slowly, but consistent self-work leads to progress. With dedication and practice, we can cultivate greater emotional intelligence and more effective anger management skills. It is best if these abilities are built into children when they are very young so it becomes an auto response as they grow up.

Chapter 8

Zen Effects

- Rose

"Dont go outside yourself, return into yourself."

- St Augustine.

The human brain is an extraordinary marvel of evolution. It operates as a super optimization machine at all times. Its complex yet intricate neural circuitry constantly seeks efficiency and coherence, processing immense amounts of information in milliseconds. However, beneath its extraordinary capabilities lies an inherent tendency for pattern recognition. From infancy, we are wired to recognise patterns in our surroundings, enabling us to navigate the complexities of existence with relative ease. For example, small children often use the word 'dog' to refer to all four-legged animals. As they grow older they start adding more and more words to this generalization. Every aspect of our life goes through this kind of generalization. Our decision-making process, which seems to be based on rational thought and careful consideration, is often influenced by unconscious patterns we have developed.

Even though we try to carefully consider our options while making a decision, our choices often follow familiar patterns shaped by past experiences, beliefs, and societal influences. These patterns strongly affect our behavior, often leading us to make familiar, but not always the best, decisions.

Many of the stressors that plague our lives find their origins in these deeply entrenched patterns of thought and behavior. Whether it be fear of failure, anxiety over uncertainty, or the relentless pursuit of perfection, these patterns have a vice-like grip on our consciousness, maintaining cycles of stress and hurdles.

Yet, just beneath the surface of our realities lie the potential for complete freedom from these perpetual traps. There lies the possibility of a journey of self-discovery and change that goes beyond our usual way of thinking. Such deep self-work requires a serious commitment to uncover and move past the conditioning that hides our true potential. It requires courage, introspection, and a willingness to confront our patterns and attachments when we notice them. Deep practices such as Falun Dafa and Vipassana Meditation offer profound opportunities for self-discovery and liberation. Falun Dafa, also known as Falun Gong is an ancient cultivation practice which helps individuals identify and escape their mental traps, leading to true liberation. To break free from the grip of our patterns, we must rewrite the narrative of our lives. We must challenge the stories we tell ourselves, questioning the validity of our beliefs and assumptions. Similarly, Vipassana Meditation involves a ten-day silent retreat that fosters deep awareness and personal growth. Both practices are taught for free all over the world, requiring only a commitment to diligent practice.

'Zhuan Falun' (freely downloadable from the website) is the core book of Falun Dafa, containing the teachings of the practice taught by the founder, Mr. Li Hongzhi. It covers various aspects of spiritual cultivation, including the principles of truthfulness, compassion, and forbearance, as well as explanations of the universe, karma, and levels of cultivation. The practice is suitable for individuals of all ages, this practice yields significant benefits right from the first day. It is simple to integrate into our daily life, requiring no specific schedule or dedicated time. With its ease of adoption, it can be practiced anytime, anywhere, throughout the day.

Embracing Emotional Mastery:

Just as we strengthen our bodies through workouts in the gym to achieve physical strength, we must also cultivate our mental resilience to confront life's adversities. Within each of us lie innate capacities that, if nurtured, can make us resilient in the face of challenges. Through mindfulness practices and emotional regulation, we harness the transformative power of our emotions, transmuting fear into courage, anger into compassion, and despair into resilience.

Finding Lasting Peace:

As we embark on this journey of deep self-work and emotional mastery, we gradually unravel the patterns that have kept us ensnared in cycles of suffering. With each layer shed, we inch closer to the elusive shores of lasting peace—a state of being that transcends the transient fluctuations of our day to day circumstances. Here, amidst the ebb and flow of life, we discover a profound sense of inner tranquility—a sanctuary that resides not in external validation or material success, but in the boundless depths of our own being.

In the intense process of deep self-work and mastering our emotions, we find the key to lasting peace. Amid the constant flow of thoughts and feelings, we discover the path to our own awakening. By understanding and breaking free from our habitual thinking patterns, we regain our natural freedom and independence. In the quiet of our own minds, we find a peace that goes beyond understanding—a timeless refuge that remains steady even in the chaos of life.

6 Tips by Kum Kum to Find Zen in Our Everyday Lives:

Happiness is a place where Zen lives.

1. Close your eyes – just shut out the world and gaze inwards. Zen is a type of Buddhism that is used to stay present and non-judgmental. Do this whenever and wherever. It's the first step towards peace.

2. Facing a stressful moment? Slow down, take deep breaths and count till 10. Can add Ujjayi breaths (an ancient yoga breathing method) to your counting. This can help us in feeling more grounded and balanced.

3. Walk or cycle instead of driving. Hold steady, look tall. Walk, Breathe. Perhaps try a bit of W.M. (Walking Meditation). Fitness walking stretches our bodies, inner walking stretches our minds

and souls. The Zen master Han-Shan said that this type of walking helps us to see our lives in totality as a whole. It helps us to be friends with ourselves, where we can think, daydream, analyze, and breathe, all this while we walk. As we pay attention to the movement of the body, we relax in our mind, there is clarity and sparks of insight. For sure, inner walking is a total experience. It's an inner game that you can practice and learn. With movement comes stillness, awareness and surrendering to the movement.

4. Wake up earlier than your fixed time. Keep a journal, meditate, work out, anything to energize and feel the gratitude in your heart.

5. Savor each moment. Learn to live in the 'Now.'

6. Practice letting go in small ways, small things, be it valuables, property you haven't inherited, a relationship gone bad, a child that has left you disappointed.

Let the feeling of Peace, Oneness, and Joy engulf you.

Chapter 9

4A's + 1

- Kum Kum

When we talk about personality, what do we mean? Is it a body, our inner being? Is it looks, beauty? Is it about confidence, self-esteem, or our body language? The way we talk, walk, sleep, sit, or stand? Does a personality reflect our views about life? How best to define a personality?

For now, let's reflect on a 'Presence,' also known as 'Spirit,' 'Essence,' or 'Rooh.' (or andar ki baat). It is not a matter of "stand up; shoulders back; tummy in;" but rather walk proudly, breathe fully and remember who you are.

1st A – Awaaz (Voice):

We humans have been blessed with an incredible variety of voice tones—singing voices, shrilly or deep ones, oratorical ones, soft and feminine ones, loud or high pitched etc. But do we always use this gift to the best of our ability? Do we use a soft, polite, clear, firm, pleasing tone or do we let ourselves get loud, harsh and high pitched?

It's okay if sometimes our voice is loud and harsh. It's natural to express our feelings. Behind an angry, loud voice, there is pain. But behind a calm voice, there is love and empathy.

If you feel like you can sing, do it as often as you can. Take up singing lessons if you want. Singing is one of the best ways to lose ourselves. It transports us into another space!

As humans, do we use our voice to communicate, scold, guide, praise, shout or show love, and compassion or as someone says, "God invented language so that human beings had a medium to complain!"

2nd A – Aankhen (Eyes):

Eyes are also known as the windows of the soul. A song says it all, *"Aankhen bhi hoti hai dil ki zubaan, bin bole kar deti hai halat bayan.*

(eyes act like the voice of the heart, without a sound everything is told!)," Again, how can we use them to the best of our ability?

- Our smiles should reach the eyes – for our eyes tell all.

- By maintaining good eye contact while communicating. See what a lover says, *"Baat karne me jo mushkil ho tumhe mehfil mein, mein samjh jaounga, nazaron se batana mujhko (If in a crowd you are hesitant to communicate, I will understand. Just let your eyes do the talking)."*

- I have always believed that a little bit of eye makeup is very essential to bring about the beauty in a woman's face. So, go ahead, experiment, and learn how to best define your eyes. There are many videos to help make you do so.

3rd A- Ang (Body):

It's not all about a fit body but a body image that matters. It's all about body language, the way we dress, look, walk, talk, sit, stand, and even lie down. Are we happy with our body image? Do we stand tall, or slouch, do we do enough to improve on all this? The 7th Habit of Stephen Covey 'Sharpen the Saw,' is just about doing this—to constantly renew, reinvent, and reshape ourselves. Even excessive hand and head movements can distract from a good body image. Do we have a confident look? A first impression can also be the last one. Dressing sense and grooming is also of utmost importance.

It is not a question of fat or slim body, just endeavor to maintain a healthy body weight. Eating right, exercising right, and thinking right all go hand in hand.

4ᵗʰ A – Adayain/Andaz (Style and Substance):

We have all heard of *"Ye qatil(deadly) adayain or ye qatilana(deadly) andaz!."* What does it really mean? Is it a poet's perception or the lover's compliments? They do say, "Beauty is in the eyes of the beholder." A song goes like this, *"Aadayain bhi hain, mohabbat bhi hai, sharafat bhi hai, mere mehboob mein, vo deewanapan, vo masoomiyat, shararat bhi hai mere mehboob mein (My lover has a certain style, an innocence, a playfulness, a craziness, a decency; she is an amalgamation of all this and more)."* We have to keep this shararat-a playful nature-alive within us.

Every woman is beautiful. She just has to discover that uniqueness within her. And that particular quality is what makes her attractive to others and to herself. Shakespeare has said, "To thine Ownself be true." Don't be afraid to be yourself- just find your USP (Unique Selling Point) - and let it reflect in your personality.

"5ᵗʰ A – Attitude (Nazariya)

Ask yourself. Are we...

1.	Optimistic or Pessimistic?	Successful, but are we happy?
2.	Listless or energetic?	Coping well with our life happenings?
3.	Smiling enough?	Living life to the fullest?
4.	Laughing often?	Taking life too seriously?
5.	Enjoying good friendships/ relationships?	Feeling lonely and neglected?

A study in Harvard University found that when a person gets a job or promotion, 85% is because of his or her attitude and 15% is his intelligence and knowledge of specific facts and figures. A good attitude is a foundation of success regardless of your chosen fields.

Shiv Khera says that attitude is the most important word in the English language! We all know the benefits of a positive attitude and drawbacks of a negative one.

> "A pessimist sees the difficulty in every opportunity. An optimist sees the opportunity in every difficulty."
>
> - Winston Churchill

Even Facebook tells us that the difference between a good day and a bad one is our attitude.

Now the question remains: CAN we build a positive attitude? Can we cultivate it?

The answer is **'YES!'** It's our choice. With a negative approach, our life is limited and narrow. But the possibilities are endless with a positive attitude.

1. Learn to be an optimist. Practice, think, and reason. Notice good things when they happen. Give yourself positive feedback. Try not to always blame yourself when things go wrong. Acknowledge your emotions and then move on.

2. Try to do it now. Don't always make excuses. Don't procrastinate.

3. Work on your self esteem. Take stock of your strengths. Tell yourself, "I may not have done this before, but I'm confident that I can and will succeed."

4. Stay away from negative influences. People who hold you down, try and keep them at bay.

5. Cultivate an Attitude of Gratitude.

6. Learn to like the things that need to be done such as errands, everyday responsibilities etc.

7. Think 'Win-Win!' Meditate on it.

8. Our attitude should be flexible, not rigid.

John Maxwell, author of Developing the Leader within You, says, "We cannot choose how many years we will live, but we can choose how much life these years will have. We cannot control the beauty of our face, but can control the expression on it. We cannot control life's difficult moments, but we can choose to make life less difficult. We cannot control the atmosphere of the world, but we can control the atmosphere of our mind. Too often we choose to control things we cannot change. Too seldom we choose to control what we can – our attitude."

> "Attitude is more important than the past, than education, than money, than circumstances, than what people do or say. It is more important than appearances, giftedness or skills."

> \- Charles R. Swindoll

Chapter 10

Expect the Unexpected

- Kum Kum

"If you do not expect the unexpected, you will not find it, for it is not to be reached by search or trial."

- Heraclitus.

Years ago, when we were posted in Patna, my husband and I had the privilege of a 24 X 7 Police Guard. My two little girls, Noura and Runa used to hang out with them, both sharing their lunch (best Dal Puri ever) or Noura posing with them in her own police uniform and cap, given to her by her grandfather, Jackie. The day we left, it was a teary eyed farewell, but never to forget the departing line of one of the guards, *"Madam, Kisi ko koi muqammal jahan nahi milta (No one ever inherits a complete world)."*

In the present day, there are earthquakes, floods, typhoons, forest fires, landslides, droughts, and many other disastrous consequences just waiting to happen due to climate change, even with entire roads disappearing.

Then came Covid, an unexpected happening!

Now, people are traveling with a vengeance, leading to delayed and canceled flights, over priced tickets, overcrowding, over selling, and over competitiveness.

Wars are going on and on while the new age gurus talk about peace and tranquility.

On a personal front too, then, let's learn to expect the unexpected.

- Having grown up in a sheltered environment, just as I was beginning to settle down, feeling a passion in my occupation in the teaching line in M.G.D., the wedding bells rang! But of course, it was the done thing in those days, leaving me with few options.

- My first pregnancy was also unexpected. We were in Cairo then, leading a diplomatic life, when we were blessed with a baby girl on the day of Diwali. We named her Noura (Light).

- Having nearly lost her at 8 months, this same child was diagnosed with cancer at the age of 13. When my father broke this news to me, the ground shifted under my feet. The truth does not always set you free. It can kill you, shake you, slice you open, and turn everything inside out, upside down. We fought the war of survival with her, till lo and behold, God's Grace and Glory shone on her. Noura was healed by the time she was 18.

- Then life held a sweet surprise for me. While in Ottawa, and after, a friendship between Noura and Ben stayed and prospered (survived over the years of parting and sorrow). Benjamin Su became our son-in-law and we inherited Taiwanese *'samdhis' (in-laws)*.

- Life went on. We moved from posting to posting, house to house, schools to schools, friends to friends. Till the 13th move, I went to a self made Bungalow in Jaipur, with a big and beautiful garden, in which I had poured my heart and soul into. My Mumbai based niece Nayanika had designed it. I worked hard to keep a well maintained and functional home.

- The hand of fate struck again. After my mother-in-law's death, we planned a trip outside the country. The last few days, we got a call from Runa, my daughter, saying that our house was burgled and all my jewelry was stolen. A young tenant who was supposed to guard the place in our absence, left and went to his village in Bengal. Some antique and stunning pieces that belonged to my mother, everything was gone! A few depressing months later, I decided to put my house up for sale, as in any case my husband was not in love with Jaipur as I was.

- Few months later, while still in Jaipur, my sister-in-law's call came as a shock! My elder brother Prakash had passed away. (He had served in the Indian Army). He was an intelligent and extremely talented man; his love for Indian music, British and Indian history, cooking, calligraphy, playing guitar, mouth organ, tabla, and flute was a hit with all his friends. His book 'An Introduction to Hindustani Classical Music' is doing well. But alas, his fondness for liquor did him in.

• Losing someone you love tunes you into the fragility of life, of moments, and memories of music. I remember when we were young, he made me listen to the maestro Madan Mohan's melodies and their nuances. Since then I have become fond of playing the harmonium and now and then, I sing a few of my favorite songs. It makes you want to grasp unplayed notes of unplayed symphonies.

• After one and a half years we were back in Delhi. This was the 14th move!

By now, I had seemed to have lost myself, for there were so many pieces of me scattered everywhere. But then I told myself: Admit, adapt, adjust and move on.

• "Sometimes you need to lose yourself to find yourself. "

• "Do not be conformed to this world, but be transformed by the renewal of your mind. Lose yourself wholly, and the more you lose, the more you will find." [Romans 12: 2]

But how do we turn inspiration to practicality? Here are some TIPS to find ourselves when we feel lost:

1. Start doing the things you love. Make a list.

2. Surround yourself with positive people (Online and in real life). Drop the ones that drain you.

3. Try new things: new hobbies, new experiences. They hold you, balance you, and sustain you. Get you out of your comfort zone.

4. Getting organized is a very 'feel-good' strategy. It never fails to energize you.

5. Realize that self-care is not selfish.

6. Set goals, small at first. Automatically, you will move forward.

7. Live in the moment. Focus on the Present.

8. Carpe diem (Seize the day). Endeavor to make use of every opportunity that comes your way. Ask yourself, "What about these circumstances, can I turn it into an opportunity?"

9. Keep a journal. Reflect.

10. Practice mindfulness. More awareness to each moment, with acceptance and without judgement, goes a long way in finding yourself.

11. Look at the larger picture. Don't sweat the small stuff. Focus on the big stuff.

12. Let it be. Intend for a certain outcome, let it go and wait for the result. Indeed life is a balance of holding on and letting go.

13. Has God loved you ever? Start seeing your blessings. Check out the strokes of luck you have had.

"The best way to find yourself is in the service of others"

- Mahatma Gandhi

Prologue

Over the last ten years in Delhi, we have much to be grateful for. Travel, family, friends, clubs, and other social gatherings. But now that one of us needs medical care and advice on a regular basis, it's best to be here, near a hospital, thereby opening the possibilities that all events have a meaning. We have to expand our vision and the reason will be revealed.

Was this the creative solution appearing out of nowhere?

Life seemed to have come full circle. This WAS in my best interest. The robbery had spurred us on to move house. Now it's each new day, each new way, new possibilities, new obstacles, new solutions, and new resolutions.

The Cruise that never was!

Having worked for nearly a year with planning, dreaming, and choosing a holiday cruise; it all fell apart. In the evening, before we were to start our holiday, one of us had to be hospitalized. Maybe at the back of my mind I expected this, but I had fooled myself by feeling excited and happy. Disappointed and disheartened, I had no choice but to cancel and cope with the new situation.

You surrender, accept and forgive.

God's plan, picture and plot into the unknown are available at every step. It is ours to know and accept. Ours to Receive.

"Trust me and plunge the jeweled dagger into your Heart."
This is what it takes to lose myself.
There is no other path back to God."

- Hafiz

"Acceptance is the answer to all my problems today. I can find no serenity until I accept the person, place, thing,or situation as being exactly the way it's supposed to be."

- Alcoholics Anonymous

IndiePress

The best route your story can take.

To publish your own book, contact us.

We publish poetry collections, short story collections, novellas and novels.

contact@http://indiepress.in/

Instagram- indie_press

www.ingramcontent.com/pod-product-compliance
Lightning Source LLC
LaVergne TN
LVHW091619170726
843492LV00007B/2501